"I Can Find God" is a wonderful, insightful, inspiring book for children of all ages – the young and the young at heart. The beautiful illustrations, combined with the easy to digest messages allows any child to understand the concept of God and allows them to see that "there is no spot where God is not."

Karen Drucker
singer/songwriter/author

Evelyn Kahrs' I Can Find God is an uplifting journey for the impressionable young mind. She has a gift for guiding her readers toward an elegant understanding of the Divine. The world will be a very different place when we all experience God in this way.

Rev. Dr. John B Waterhouse
President, Centers for Spiritual Living

ISBN: 978-1-4525-6385-5 (sc)
ISBN: 978-1-4525-6386-2 (e)

Library of Congress Control Number: 2013900092

Balboa Press books may be ordered through booksellers or by contacting:

Balboa Press
A Division of Hay House
1663 Liberty Drive
Bloomington, IN 47403
www.balboapress.com
1-(877) 407-4847

Printed in the United States of America

Balboa Press rev. date: 1/7/2013

BALBOA
PRESS
A DIVISION OF HAY HOUSE

I CAN FIND GOD

Evelyn Kahrs

Illustrator – Linda M Brandt

Balboa Press

A Division of Hay House

Dedication

With thanks to our four children,
David, Carole, Cindy & Elizabeth, who
introduced me many years ago to the
joy to be found in children's books.

Where can I find God?
I can find God...

In the grass and in the trees
In the birds and in the bees

In the flowers and
in the weeds

In the tiniest little seeds

In the snow and in the rain

In the mountains, on the plains

In rivers and ponds all over the land

In each
mosquito and
butterfly

In turtles, frogs,
and lizards small

In fish that swim and
snakes that crawl

In alligators, bears, and
very large whales

In camels,
elephants,
and monkeys
with tails

In horses,
cows, chickens,
and hogs

In brothers, sisters, aunts, uncles, and cousins

All ages, all
colors, all sizes
– there's dozens

God is in me, God is in you

Wherever we are,
God is there too.

Where can I find God?
God is found in every spot
There is no spot where God is not!***
I can find God EVERYWHERE!

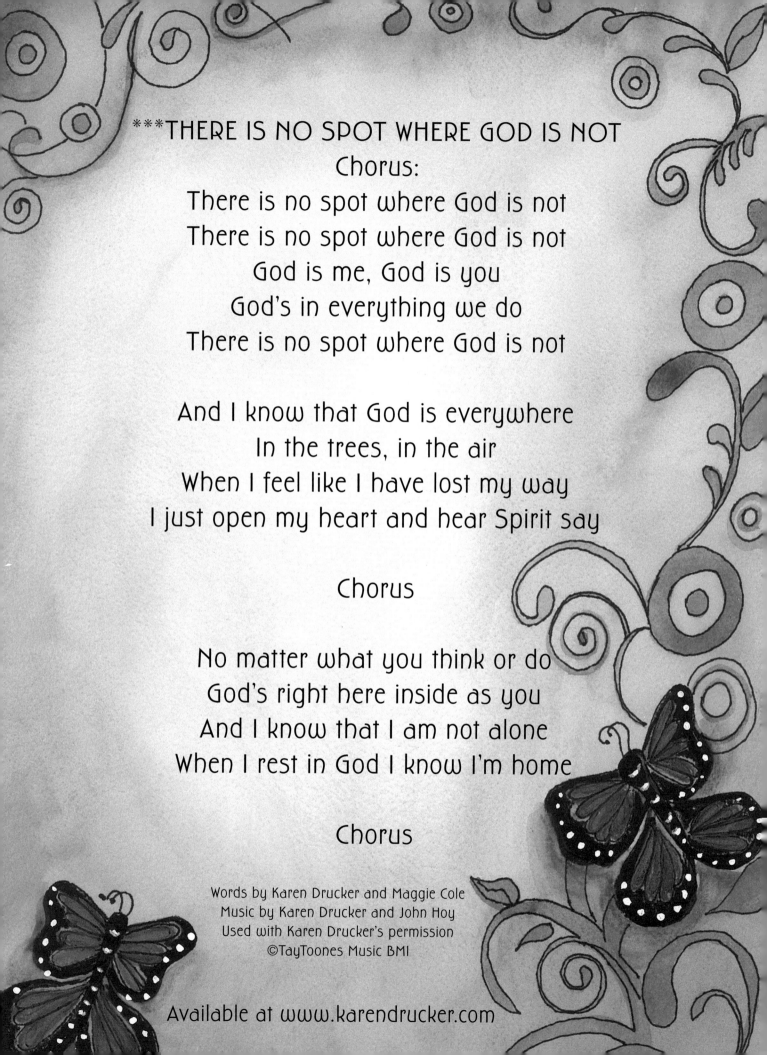

***THERE IS NO SPOT WHERE GOD IS NOT
Chorus:
There is no spot where God is not
There is no spot where God is not
God is me, God is you
God's in everything we do
There is no spot where God is not

And I know that God is everywhere
In the trees, in the air
When I feel like I have lost my way
I just open my heart and hear Spirit say

Chorus

No matter what you think or do
God's right here inside as you
And I know that I am not alone
When I rest in God I know I'm home

Chorus

Words by Karen Drucker and Maggie Cole
Music by Karen Drucker and John Hoy
Used with Karen Drucker's permission
©TayToones Music BMI

Available at www.karendrucker.com

Printed in the United States
by Baker & Taylor Publisher Services